Tactical Journal

Gina Guy-Warren

First Printing
The Word and the Workout.™
Prophetic Insight into Physical, Emotional & Spiritual Fitness
Tactical Journal

Published by Unbreakable Reed, LLC

"A broken reed He will not break, and a dimly burning wick He will not quench; He will bring forth justice in truth." (Isaiah 42:3 AMPCE)

Cover and interior design: Kristen Ingebretson

ISBN: 978-0-578-50945-7

Printed in the United States of America

To all who've been misunderstood,
rejected and told your voice doesn't matter.

Your words were displaced only for a season but will now find a place upon the pages of this journal.

God is listening; start speaking. . . .

HOW TO USE THE **TACTICAL JOURNAL**

The military term *tactical* means to maneuver or a plan of action that is designed toward gaining a desired end or temporary advantage, or actions carefully planned to gain a specific military end. If we don't have a plan of action, we will continue to circle around the same obstacles year after year. In addition, a compass, a computerized movement planning and status system, is used for direction. We are in need of both strategic planning and clear direction if we are going to take back our destinies! It's time to break the cycle!

As I look back at my own life and examine both patterns and cycles, I can see how connections with people, events, and places have become a road map for my future. If we pay attention to the road maps of our lives, we will see how everything connects. From the places we have been, to people who come in and out of our lives, every piece fits within the frame of the puzzle. We know in part and we see in part, but as we gather all the "parts" of our journey, and begin to put all of them in perspective, we will have clearer direction for our futures. I hear so many people say they have no idea what their purpose is and they feel so lost. If you are someone who feels lost, and you don't understand your position–look back! How has the enemy attacked you throughout your life? The Bible tells us our steps are ordered by the Lord; so if we can look at where we have been, we will have greater understanding of where we are headed!

Each day in this thirty-day tactical journal begins with a word of wisdom that the Holy Spirit has spoken to my heart for you. Use it to trace the footsteps of your life–both good, bad, and even what may appear to be inconsequential. You, too, will begin to see your purpose and understand a little clearer where your future is headed!

DAY 1

Unforgiveness is a terrorist threat to the heart.

DAY 2

The word of God never changes, but the times do. His methods may surprise you.

DAY 3

You will make mistakes, but your mistakes never make who you are.

DAY 4

I would rather walk the road of the unknown than sit on the wall of known complacency.

DAY 5

Focused accuracy will save your day, and the choices you make now will affect your tomorrow.

DAY 6

Courage belongs to those who step out into uncertainty in order to obey their God.

DAY 7

People are not a waste of time;
however, people can waste your time.

DAY 8

Tides are turning. Evil will recede due to bold believers speaking truth.

DAY 9

If we are not careful, we will think God is refining someone other than ourselves.

DAY 10

Transparency is the vein in which his glory travels.

DAY 11

The overlooked are about to move to the front lines and be seen. They recognized you at first glance but didn't give you another thought. They will now.

DAY 12

For the sake of others, sanctify yourself. You must give your life away to free the lives of others.

DAY 13

Real unity sees past one's weaknesses and into the heart of the matter.

DAY 14

Never give up, but always give in.

DAY 15

God works in the spiritual realm where nothing of valuable is ever lost or wasted.

DAY 16

Meditation is the act of keeping our thoughts, which ultimately translate into our actions, upon God's laws.

DAY 17

A broken heart is a sign you're about to be used mightily.

DAY 18

We are called to empower others, not overpower them.

DAY 19

Truth must be mixed lavishly with love.

DAY 20

Every trial and hardship has equipped you to move forward. You're now armed and ready to advance.

DAY 21

Freedom of speech is no longer free,
and it will cost you something.
Are you willing to pay the price?

DAY 22

Expectation and perfection blind us from experiencing joy in the process.

DAY 23

Waiting is not a sign of weakness but of maturity.

DAY 24

Religious people place opinions and principles above the needs of the person.

DAY 25

The people you can trust are the ones who help you perform at your best.

DAY 26

There are times to pray and times to act. Evil prevails when good men do nothing and stand by.

DAY 27

Tolerance is the ability or willingness to accept the existence of opinions or behavior that one does not necessarily agree with.

DAY 28

Grace without love breeds condemnation and shame.

DAY 29

My people seek deliverance, but I require discipline.

DAY 30

Your current circumstances do not change His promises; they just prepare you to receive them.

ABOUT THE AUTHOR

Gina Guy-Warren has served in full-time ministry for more than twenty-five years and is the founder of Truth-N-Love Ministry International. She and her husband, Brian Warren, MMA Fight Champion, defend, mobilize, train, and equip those who have been hurt by life and religion. Gina is a confidant to many leaders who suffer in private and is a revivalist teaching how to move in the Holy Spirit. She founded The Word and the Workout, which is a unique fitness ministry that combines physical fitness with focused discipline, and she has also trained Homeland Security personnel. Gina has traveled throughout many countries in Africa, including South Sudan as Vice-president of International Relief, founding a school in the Congo. She was instrumental in the healing of the Congolese people after the genocide between Rwanda/Congo, all while working medical clinics. She implemented entrepreneur workshops for the widows and teachers. Gina is the mother of two daughters and Brian's daughter. Gina and Brian currently reside in Franklin, Tennessee.

facebook.com/TruthNLoveMinistryInternational
twitter.com/ProphetGinaGuy
instagram.com/wordandtheworkout/truthnloveministry/Mrunbreakable22

ALSO BY THE WARRENS

Book One of The Word and the Workout Series
Prophetic Insight Into Physical, Emotional, & Spiritual Fitness
The Way of a Warrior

The church is in serious trouble! Many people in the pews are fighting personal battles: PTSD, mental illness, anxiety, and depression, while candy-coated, inspirational teachings infiltrate pulpits across America and innocent people are caught in the crossfire.

In this thirty-day devotional study, Gina Guy-Warren offers unique, biblical insight regarding the condition of the church today. From false teachings, medications, the foods we consume, to social media, Gina holds nothing back. She shares from personal life lessons as well as prophetic revelation she's received from the Father. From the White House, courthouse, to the church house, God's cleaning house!

Through *The Way of a Warrior* you will learn how to look back at your past battles and recognize the people, places, and events that have influenced your life today. Now is the time for all warriors who have been broken on the battlefield of life to be healed and restored. You canbe set free once and for all in every area!

Unbreakable Love is the story of one man's unbreakable love for his daughter, and about God's unbreakable love for him, despite his faults and failings as a man. Known as Mr. Unbreakable in the ring and cage, Brian Warren has delivered by earning two title belts and battling some of the best fighters in the world, including UFC fighters Cung Le, Karo Parisyan, and Ben Saunders. And though Brian hasn't always won—in life or the ring—his spirit remains unbreakable. This is a story of courage, unwavering devotion, and determination to rise from the ashes and to stand once again as a champion, and this time for the glory of God and his beloved daughter, Breesa. Brian's story will inspire you to be a better man, father, and disciple, and to never give up on yourself and certainly not on your dreams.

Available on Amazon. Pick up a copy today.

Made in the USA
Coppell, TX
16 December 2021

68961003R00039